P9-BZG-222

IRISH
BLESSINGS

An Illustrated Edition

With Legends, Poems
&
Greetings

Illustrated by Clair Moritz

KILKENNY PRESS
New York

This 1990 edition is published by Kilkenny Press, distributed by Outlet Book Company, Inc., a Random House Company,
225 Park Avenue South, New York, New York 10003, by arrangement with Windsor Communications Group, Inc.

Book design by Clair Moritz

Manufactured in Singapore

Library of Congress Cataloging-in-Publication Data
Irish blessings : with legends, poems & greetings / drawings by Clair Moritz.
p. cm.
ISBN 0-517-69688-6
1. Folk literature. Irish—Translations into English. 2. English literature—Translations from Irish. 3. English literature—Irish authors. 4. Ireland—Literary collections.
[PB1421.175 1990]
398.2′09415—dc20 89-28032
CIP

10 9 8 7 6 5 4 3

FOREWORD

Love of life, fierce pride in national heritage, strong religious belief, a sparkling sense of humor—all of these are qualities associated with the Irish people. And they are no better represented than here in this collection of Irish blessings, legends, poems, and greetings.

Many of the special blessings included in this volume have been adapted from the Breastplate of St. Patrick—these are largely inspirational and reflect the intense religious nature of the Irish. But the wit and impish qualities for which the Irish are so well known are also here: "May you be half an hour in Heaven before the Devil knows you're dead" is just one such example.

"The Legend of the Shamrock," "The Legend of the Blarney Stone," and "The Legend of the Leprechaun" best express Irish traditional wisdom, folklore, and superstition. These legends are time and again referred to and repeated in Irish literature as well as in day-to-day living.

The Irish pride in nature, heritage, and language—a trait that influenced many Irish poets—is also well represented. Selections from Thomas Moore and others are included.

But the anonymous writer who penned "If you're lucky enough to be Irish . . . you're lucky enough" best expresses the feeling of the blessings and poems collected in this book. So, even if you're *not* Irish, the charm, spirit, and soul of these people is strong enough here for all to experience. Whether for use in wishing someone well or just plain reading, this book is meant for everyone to share. Enjoy it, and "May good luck be with you wherever you go, and your blessings outnumber the shamrocks that grow."

KITTY NASH

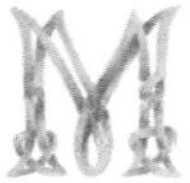

May the good saints protect you
And bless you today
And may trouble ignore you
Each step of the way.

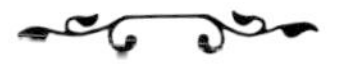

May joy and peace surround you,
Contentment latch your door,
And happiness be with you now
And bless you evermore.

May the saints protect ye—
An' sorrow neglect ye,
An' bad luck to the one
That doesn't respect ye
t' all that belong to ye,
An' long life t' yer honor—
That's the end of my song t' ye!

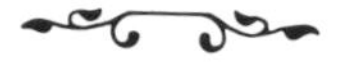

May good luck be your friend
In whatever you do
And may trouble be always
A stranger to you.

May your blessings outnumber
The shamrocks that grow
And may trouble avoid you
Wherever you go.

These things I warmly wish for you—
Someone to love,
Some work to do,
A bit o' sun
A bit o' cheer
And a guardian angel
Always near.

An Old Irish Greeting

Wherever there is happiness
Hope you'll be there too,
Wherever there are friendly smiles
Hope they'll smile on you,
Wherever there is sunshine,
Hope it shines especially
For you to make each day for you
As bright as it can be.

THE LEGEND OF THE SHAMROCK

Long ago, when Ireland was the land of Druids, there was a great Bishop, Patrick by name, who came to teach the word of God throughout the country. . . . This saint, for he was indeed a saint, was well loved everywhere he went. One day, however, a group of his followers came to him and admitted that it was difficult for them to believe in the doctrine of the Holy Trinity.

Saint Patrick reflected a moment and then, stooping down, he plucked a leaf from the shamrock and held it before them, bidding them to behold the living example of the "Three-in-One." The simple beauty of this explanation convinced these skeptics, and from that day the shamrock has been revered throughout Ireland.

May your troubles be less
And your blessings be more
And nothing but happiness
Come through your door.

IRELAND

It's the one place on earth
That Heaven has kissed
With melody, mirth
And meadow and mist.

ay brooks and trees and singing hills
Join in the chorus too,
And every gentle wind that blows
Send happiness to you.

Lucky stars above you,
Sunshine on your way,
Many friends to love you,
Joy in work and play —
Laughter to outweigh each care,
In your heart a song—
And gladness waiting everywhere
All your whole life long!

May you never find trouble
All crowdin' and shovin'
But always good fortune—
All smilin' and lovin'.

May good luck be with you
Wherever you go,
And your blessings outnumber
The shamrocks that grow.

henever I dream, it seems I dream
Of Erin's rolling hills—
Of all its lovely, shimmery lakes
And little babbling rills—
I hear a colleen's lilting laugh
Across a meadow fair
And in my dreams it almost seems
To me that I am there—
O, Ireland! O, Ireland!
We're never far apart
For you and all your beauty
Fill my mind and touch my heart.

E. Gary Brooks

With the first light of sun—
Bless you
When the long day is done—
Bless you
In your smiles and your tears—
Bless you
Through each day of your years—
Bless you.

You've blessed me with friends
and laughter and fun
With rain that's as soft
as the light from the sun—
You've blessed me with stars
to brighten each night
You've given me help
to know wrong from right—
You've given me so much
please, Lord give me too,
A heart that is always
Grateful to you.

AN IRISH PRAYER

ay you always have these
blessings . . .
A soft breeze when summer comes–
A warm fireside in winter
And always—the warm, soft smile
of a friend.

May this home and all therein
be blessed with God's love.

A Special Blessing

hrist be with me,
Christ within me,
Christ behind me, Christ before me,
Christ beside me, Christ to win me,
Christ to comfort and restore me,
Christ beneath me, Christ above me,
Christ in quiet, Christ in danger,
Christ in hearts of all that love me,
Christ in mouth of friend and stranger.

FROM THE BREASTPLATE OF SAINT PATRICK

Like the warmth of the sun
And the light of the day,
May the luck of the Irish
Shine bright on your way.

Deep peace of the running waves
to you.
Deep peace of the flowing air to you.
Deep peace of the smiling stars to you.
Deep peace of the quiet earth to you.
Deep peace of the watching shepherds
to you.
Deep peace of the Son of Peace to you.

An Old Gaelic Prayer

Grant me a sense of humor, Lord,
The saving grace to see a joke,
To win some happiness from life,
And pass it on to other folk.

or the great Gaels of Ireland
Are the men that God made mad,
For all their wars are merry
And all their songs are sad.

G. K. CHESTERTON

May the lilt of Irish laughter
Lighten every load,
May the mist of Irish magic
Shorten every road,
May you taste the sweetest pleasures
That fortune ere bestowed,
And may all your friends remember
All the favors you are owed.

May you be half an hour in Heaven
Before the Devil knows you're dead.

O, Ireland isn't it grand you look—
Like a bride in her rich adornin'
And with all the pent-up love of
my heart
I bid you the top o' the mornin'.

JOHN LOCKE

May your pockets be heavy—
Your heart be light
And may good luck pursue you
Each morning and night.

May the road rise to meet you.
May the wind be always at your back.
May the sun shine warm upon your face;
The rains fall soft upon your fields
And, until we meet again,
May God hold you in the palm of His hand.

A GAELIC BLESSING

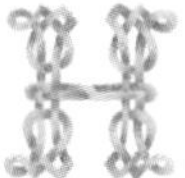
ow sweetly lies old Ireland
Emerald green beyond the foam,
Awakening sweet memories,
Calling the heart back home.

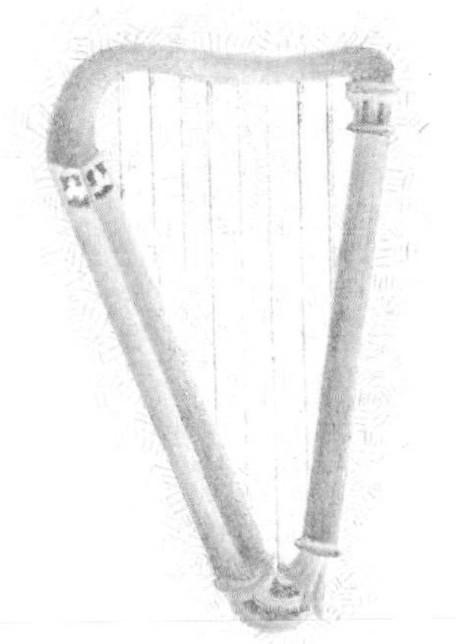

The harp that once through
Tara's halls
The soul of music shed,
Now hangs as mute on Tara's walls
As if that soul were fled
So sleeps the pride of former days,
So Glory's thrill is o'er;
And hearts that once
Beat high for praise
Now feel that pulse no more.

THOMAS MOORE

Hills as green as emeralds
Cover the countryside
Lakes as blue as sapphires—
Are Ireland's special pride.
And rivers that shine like silver
Make Ireland look so fair—
But the friendliness of her people
Is the richest treasure there.

ERIN

Where the wind has a sound like a
soft sweet song,
And anyone can hum it,
And heather grows upon the hills
And shamrocks not far from it.

May the luck of the Irish be always
at hand
And good friends always near you—
May each and every coming day
Bring some special joy to cheer you.

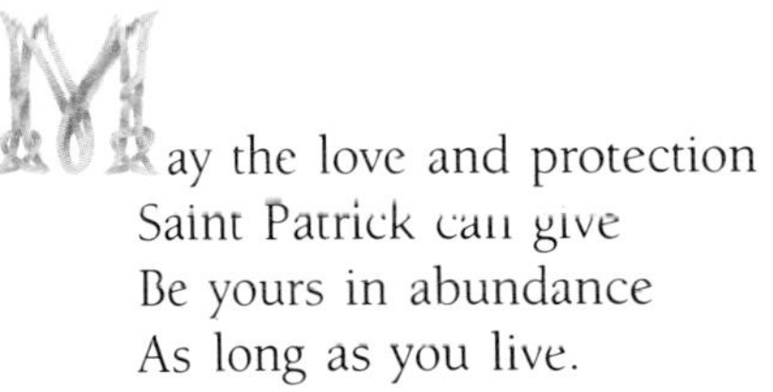

May the love and protection
Saint Patrick can give
Be yours in abundance
As long as you live.

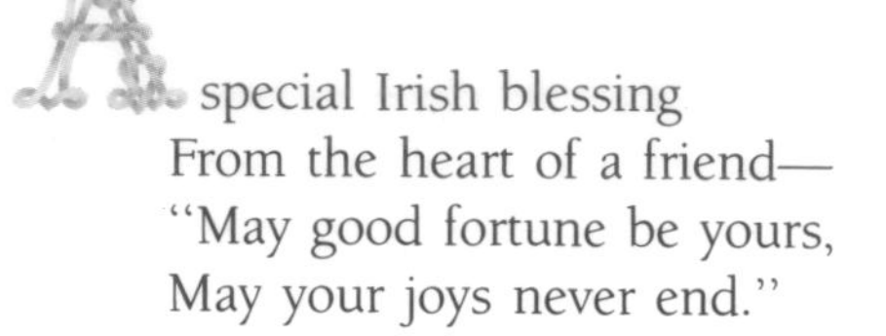

A special Irish blessing
From the heart of a friend—
"May good fortune be yours,
May your joys never end."

The rose and the shamrock
Will always remind me
Of lanes in the hills
That I left far behind me.

E. GARY BROOKS

ay your home be filled with laughter
May your pockets be filled with gold
And may you have all the happiness
Your Irish heart can hold.

A BLESSING FOR YOU AND YOURS

ay the grace of God's protection
And His great love abide
Within your home—within the hearts
Of all who dwell inside.

Take me home to Shamrock Hill
The glorious place of my birth
Where the glens are green and the
heather grows—
'Tis the prettiest place on earth—
The wind blows free and the air is fresh
And I still hear a rippling rill.
My heart is sad, but it could be glad—
Take me home to Shamrock Hill.

E. Gary Brooks

May you have all the happiness
And luck that life can hold—
And at the end of all your rainbows
May you find a pot of gold.

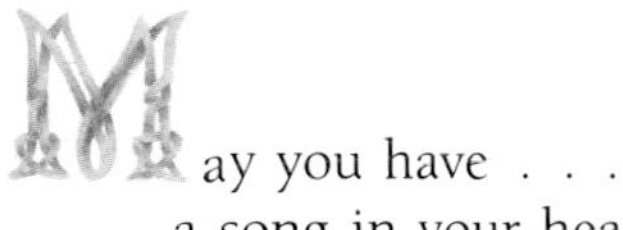

May you have . . .
a song in your heart
a smile on your lips
and nothing but joy
at your finger tips!

May your blessings be many
The sunshine above you,
Your life bring you gladness—
And always . . . God love you!

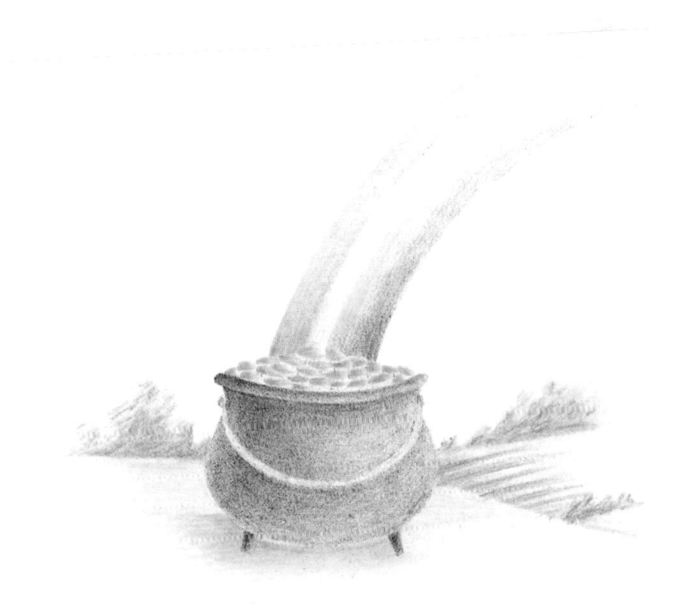

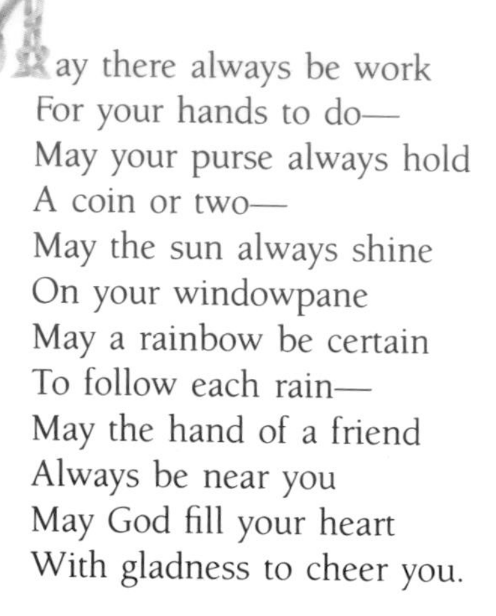

May there always be work
For your hands to do—
May your purse always hold
A coin or two—
May the sun always shine
On your windowpane
May a rainbow be certain
To follow each rain—
May the hand of a friend
Always be near you
May God fill your heart
With gladness to cheer you.

May you be blessed
with the strength of heaven—
the light of the sun and the
radiance of the moon
the splendor of fire—
the speed of lightning—
the swiftness of wind—
the depth of the sea—
the stability of earth and the firmness
of rock.

FROM THE BREASTPLATE OF SAINT PATRICK

Come and take pot-luck with me
My hearth is warm, my friendship's free.

THE BLESSING OF LIGHT

May the blessing of Light be on you, light without and light within. May the blessed sunlight shine on you and warm your heart till it glows like a great peat fire, so that the stranger may come and warm himself at it, and also a friend.

May the good saints protect ye
And the devil neglect ye!

Wishing you a rainbow
For sunlight after showers—
Miles and miles of Irish smiles
For golden happy hours—
Shamrocks at your doorway
For luck and laughter too,
And a host of friends that never ends
Each day your whole life through!

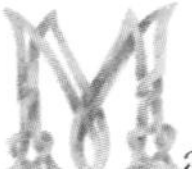ay your heart be warm and happy
With the lilt of Irish laughter
Every day in every way
And forever and ever after!

Let's all put on our dancin' shoes
And wear our shamrocks green
And toast our friends both here
and there
And everywhere between.

Like the gold of the sun,
Like the light of the day,
May the luck of the Irish
Shine bright on your way—
Like the glow of a star
And the lilt of a song
May these be your joys
All your life long.

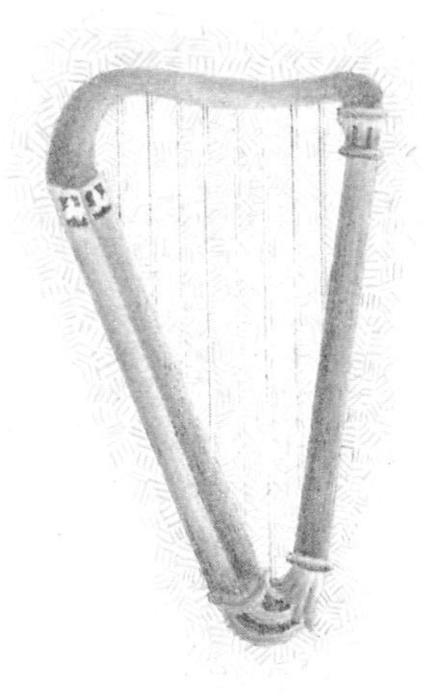

May the blessings and love
Of Saint Patrick fall
On yourself, on your home,
On your dear ones and all.

THE LEGEND OF THE LEPRECHAUN

If you should be walking along a wooded path some moonlit night in Spring and hear the faint tap-tapping of a tiny hammer, you might be lucky enough to catch a glimpse of an Irish leprechaun, the elfin shoemaker, whose roguish tricks are the delight of Irish story-telling.

According to legend, the leprechaun has a pot of gold hidden somewhere, and he must give up his treasure to the one who catches him. You'll have to step lively and think quickly to capture a leprechaun's gold though, because this sly little fellow will fool you into looking away for an instant while he escapes into the forest.

A story is told of the man who compelled a leprechaun to take him to the very bush where the gold was buried. The man tied a red handkerchief to the bush in order to recognize the spot again and ran home for a spade. He was gone only three minutes, but when he returned to dig, there was a red handkerchief on every bush in the field. As long as there are Irishmen to believe in the "little folk," there will be leprechauns to reflect the wonderful Irish sense of fun, and many a new story of leprechaun shenanigans will be added to Irish folklore each year.

God's might to direct me
God's power to protect me
God's wisdom for learning
God's eye for discerning
God's ear for my hearing
God's word for my clearing
God's hand for my cover
God's path to pass over
God's buckler to guide me
God's army to ward me.

FROM THE BREASTPLATE
OF SAINT PATRICK

I asked a leprechaun to bring
A pot of gold to you,
I asked a fiddler if he'd play
Your favorite ditty too,
I asked the saints to walk with you
Each step along the way,
And now I'm asking you to have
A very happy day!

May the blessing of light be
upon you,
light without and light within . . .
And in all your comings and goings,
may you ever have a kindly greeting
from them you meet along the road.

FROM AN OLD GAELIC PRAYER

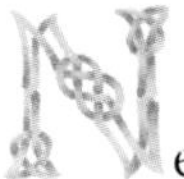ear a misty stream in Ireland
In the hollow of a tree
Live mystical, magical leprechauns
Who are clever as can be.
With their pointed ears, and turned up toes
And little coats of green
The leprechauns busily make their shoes
And try hard not to be seen.
Only those who really believe
Have seen these little elves
And if we are all believers
We can surely see for ourselves.

Here's a special Irish wish
You can hear it in Cork or Kerry—
"God bless yourself, God bless
your house,
And may your days be merry!"

As He brought new faith to Ireland
So may He bring to you,
A touch of Irish happiness
In everything you do—
And like the good Saint Patrick
May your home and life be blessed
With all God's special favors
That make you happiest.

I ARISE TODAY

Through God's strength to
pilot me,
God's might to uphold me
God's wisdom to guide me,
God's eye to look before me,
God's shield to protect me,
God's host to save me
From snares of devils,
From everyone who wishes me ill
Afar and anear
Alone and in a multitude.

FROM THE BREASTPLATE
OF SAINT PATRICK

There's music in the Irish names—
Kilkenny . . . Tipperary . . .
There's beauty in the countryside,
From Cork to Londonderry,
And whoever makes his earthly home
Close to the Irish sod
Has found a bit of Heaven
And walks hand in hand with God.

May God guard you through each
night and day
And ever watch above you . . .
God smile on everything you do.
God go with you . . . God love you!

ay good Saint Patrick bless you
And keep you in his care,
And may Our Lord be near you
To answer every prayer.

ishing you always
A bright sky above
The pleasure of doing
The things that you love—
God's blessing around you,
His light from on high,
And deeper contentment
As each day goes by.

May the hinges of our friendship never grow rusty.

AN OLD IRISH TOAST

May God in His wisdom
And infinite love
Look down on you always
From Heaven above.
May He send you good fortune
Contentment and peace
And may all your blessings
Forever increase.

God needed laughter in the world,
So he made the Irish race,
For they can meet life with a smile
And turn a happy face.

May God bless you now and always
With the gift of Irish cheer,
So you will have a happy heart
Every day— all year!

Long live the Irish!
Long live their cheer!
Long live our friendship
Year after year!

AN OLD IRISH TOAST

May you have the joy that's due you,
May the years be gracious to you,
May a blue sky smile above you,
And through all your days—
God love you!

May good Saint Patrick bring you
Each blessing that endures
And may his spirit evermore
Abide with you and yours.

I just want to say
It's a joy to address you
As Irish folks do
"May heaven bless you!"

May the patron Saint of Ireland
Be close to you each day
To bless you with good fortune
In a very special way.

It would take more lucky shamrocks
Than Ireland ever grew
To bring the luck and gladness
That I'm always wishing you.

Take all the many shamrocks
Growin' green on Erin's isle.
Take all the lilting Irish tunes
And every Irish smile,
Just add them all together
And you'll find they're quite a few
But surely not as many
As my special thoughts of you.

I wish you lots of good luck
No matter what the day
I wish you lots of sunshine
And not a bit of gray . . .
I wish you lots of laughter
And never one wee sigh,
And I hope no gift of fortune
May ever pass you by.

As sure as the shamrocks are growing
In the land which the Irish all love,
As sure as the lakes of Killarney
Reflect the blue heavens above—
As sure as the warmhearted Irish
All pay honor to Saint Patrick too,
I'm wishing you "top o' the morning"
And happiness, always, for you.

Irish wishes are prayers indeed,
And this is especially true,
When the Irish wishes are made
and sent
On any day to you.

May all the joy that echoes through
A happy Irish song
And all the luck the shamrock brings
Be yours the whole year long—
May you have blessings, pleasures, friends,
To gladden all life's way,
And may Saint Patrick smile on you
Today and every day.

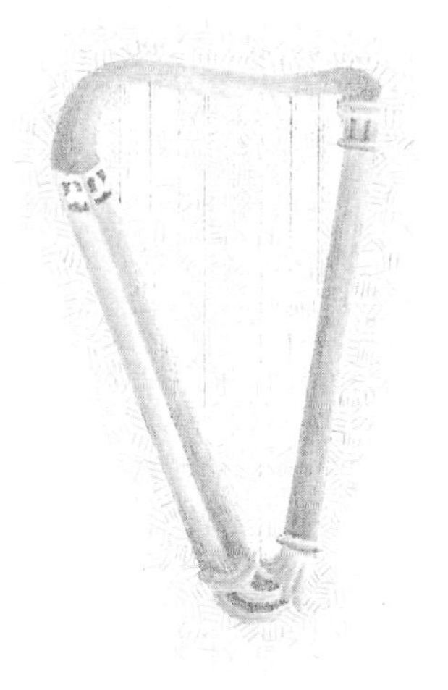

All the little leprechauns
In Ireland's sunny isle
Couldn't bring you all the luck
I'm wishing you the while.

May you always be wearing a big,
happy smile
And really enjoying each day
And may all of the luck of the Emerald Isle
Always be coming your way.

Sure and this just isn't blarney
For what I say is true—
The luck of the Irish was with me
The day that I met you.

There's the joy of old Killarney
In these wishes meant for you,
There's a bit of Irish blarney,
There's a touch of magic too—
There's a wish for lots of laughter
And good luck (be sure of that)
And a wish that all you're wishing
May come true in no time flat.

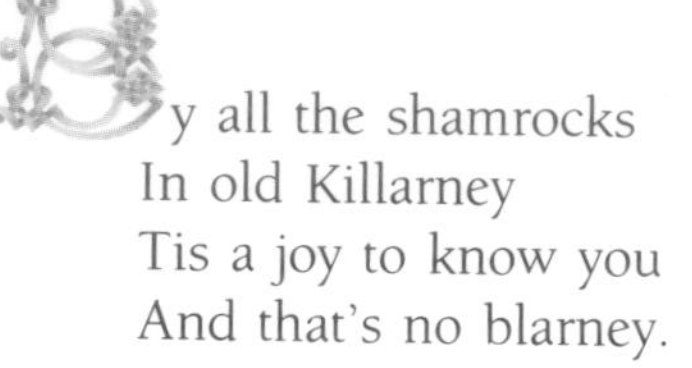

By all the shamrocks
In old Killarney
Tis a joy to know you
And that's no blarney.

May good luck befriend you,
And kind fortune send you
Whatever your heart may be wishin'
May good friends be near you
To gladden and cheer you,
And help you attain each ambition.

Wishing you joys that are lasting
and true
A heart that's not troubled or gray—
Friends who will travel life's pathway
with you
And the luck of the Irish each day.

May all your skies be blue ones
May all your dreams be seen,
May all your friends be true ones
And all your joys complete—
May happiness and laughter
Fill all your days for you
Today and ever after
May all your dreams come true.

A happy, generous nature,
A friendly spirit too—
These are the gifts Saint Patrick
Has surely given you—
And may every day to come
Bring a generous part
Of all the happy things in life
That keep joy in your heart.

THE LEGEND OF THE BLARNEY STONE

For many centuries, as everyone knows, English monarchs tried to impose their will on Ireland. Queen Elizabeth I, eager to extend the influence of her government, sent a deputy to Cormac MacDermot MacCarthy who was Lord of Blarney and demanded that he take the tenure of his lands from the Crown. Cormac set out to visit the Queen and plead for his traditional right to his land, but he despaired of success for he was not fluent of speech.

Shortly after starting his journey, he met an old woman who asked him why he looked so forlorn. He told her his story and she said, "Cormac, when Blarney Castle was built, one stone was put into place by a man who predicted no one would ever be able to touch it again. If you can kiss that stone, the gift of eloquence will be conferred upon you."

Cormac succeeded in kissing the stone and was able to address the Queen with speech so soft and words so fair that as long as he lived he never had to renounce his right to his land.

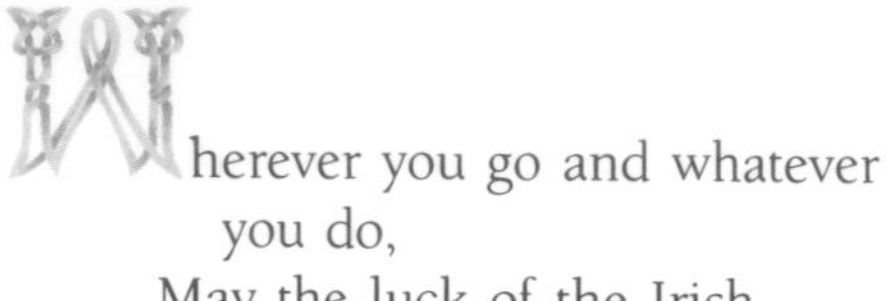

Wherever you go and whatever
you do,
May the luck of the Irish
Be there with you.

They talk of the luck of the Irish
The magic of shamrocks too,
But sure and it's more than Irish luck
To be knowing someone like you.

Like the shamrocks of Old Ireland
May your joys grow all year
through—
And Irish luck and laughter
Be a part of all you do.

Irish luck's proverbial,
It never fails, they say,
And that's the kind I'm wishin' you,
With all my heart today,
And faith, that's not the half of it,
I wish you fun and laughter
Good friends and health and happiness
Today and ever after

Wishing you lots of Irish luck
And joy in whatever life sends
Liking you always because you are you
And happy because we are friends.

Tis the best of good fortune
I hope you will know
And the best of good cheer
As the years come and go—
Good friends ever near you,
Good luck to you too,
And good health to enjoy
All I'm wishing for you.

It's a bit o' Irish luck
With all its fun and cheer
That's wished for you not just today
But every day all year.

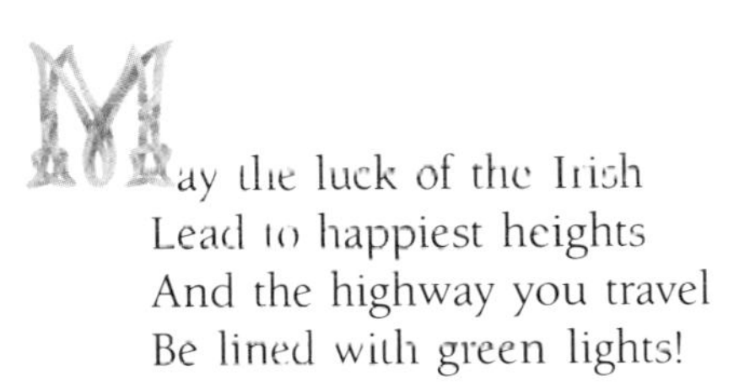

May the luck of the Irish
Lead to happiest heights
And the highway you travel
Be lined with green lights!

Here's wishing you the tops o' life
Without a single tumble
Here's wishing you the smiles o' life
And not a single grumble
Here's wishing you the best o' life
And not a flaw about it,
Here's wishing you all the joy in life
And not a day without it!

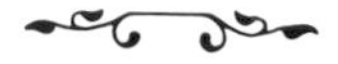

Here's to the land of the Shamrock
Where Irish hearts are true
Here's to our blessed Saint Patrick
But most of all, here's to you!

You've heard of the luck o' the Irish
It's the best in the world, no end,
And my own is the luck o' the Irish
In havin' you for my friend.

I'm wishing you joy,
I'll be havin' you know,
And the luck o' the Irish
Wherever you go.

There's a dear little plant that grows
in our isle
'Twas Saint Patrick himself sure
that set it
And the sun on his labor with pleasure
did smile,
And a tear from his eye oft-times wet it.
It grows through the bog, through the brake,
through the mireland.
And they call it the dear little Shamrock of
Ireland.

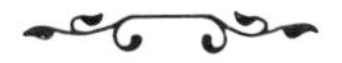

It's always the Irish who share their
last penny
With someone who's hungry for bacon
and beans
The Irish are there when it comes to a
handout
Even though it might take the last cent in
their jeans—

Big-hearted and kindly they never grow
weary
Of adding bright touches to life's somber
hue
This old world would be truly lonely and
dreary
Without 'em—God bless 'em—those real
folks like you!

All the luck o' the Irish
I'm happy to send you
With a wish that good fortune
And joy may attend you.

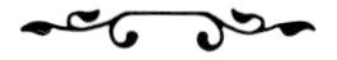

May God grant you many years to live
For sure He must be knowing
The earth has angels all too few
And Heaven is overflowing.

To wish you top of the morning
The best that any day sends
To wish you the cheer at noontime
That comes with the thought of friends—
And when the evening shadows
Fall lengthening o'er the way,
To wish you the heart's contentment
That comes with a perfect day.

Many blessings to cheer you
Each day the year through
And the luck of the Irish
In all that you do.

There are millions of shamrocks
On Erin's green isle
Thousands of Irishmen
Wearing a smile—
Hundreds of Irish lakes
Sparkling blue
But only one wonderful
Person like you.

May you always be wearin'
A big happy smile
And really enjoying each day
And may all the luck of the Emerald Isle
Always be coming your way.

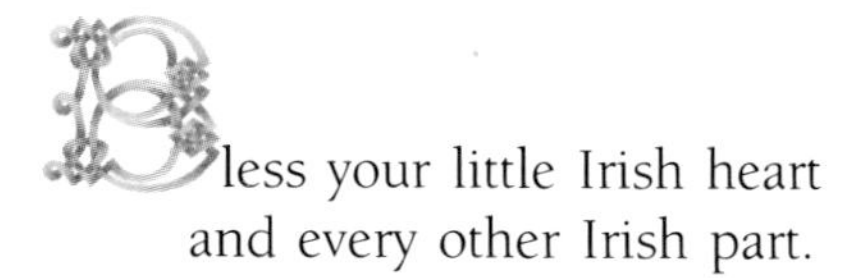

Bless your little Irish heart
and every other Irish part.

If you're lucky enough to be Irish
you're lucky enough.

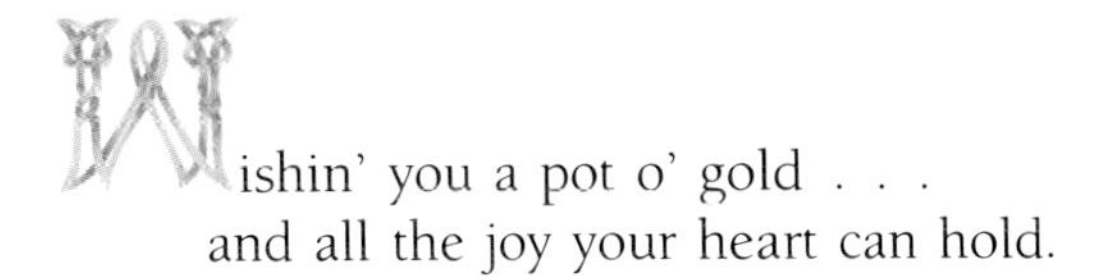

Wishin' you a pot o' gold . . .
and all the joy your heart can hold.

You'd have to look the world around
From here to old Killarney
To find someone as nice as you
And that's no Irish blarney.

God bless you—now and always—
With the gift of Irish cheer
God give to you a happy heart
And keep you through the year.

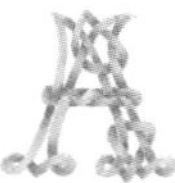

A wish that every day for you
Will be happy from the start
And may you always have good luck
And a song within your heart.

The Irish are the luckiest—
Or so I have been told,
Because at every rainbow's end
They find a pot o' gold.
So somewhere deep inside me
I must be Irish too—
For waiting at my rainbow's end
I luckily found you.

May leprechauns strew happiness
Wherever you walk each day
And Irish angels smile on you
All along the way.

In the name of old Erin
Here's wishing you cheer,
Good luck and good fortune
For many a year.

ere's a wish for a day
That's lucky all through
From the likes o' me
To the likes o' you.

May your thoughts be as glad as
the shamrocks
May your heart be as light as a song,
May each day bring you bright, happy hours
That stay with you all the year long.

As sure as there are leprechauns
To make a wish come true,
Tis nothing but the happiest
Of days I'm wishing you.

May you have lots of happiness
And Irish luck too—
May your blessings be many
And your troubles be few.

May joy be your companion
Through each and every day
Bringing lots of Irish luck
And happiness your way.

Here's hoping your face
Is wearing a smile
As cheery and bright
As the old Emerald Isle
And may a full measure
Of Irish luck too
Make each day of the year
A grand one for you.

To wish you the luck o' the Irish,
begorra!
Not just for today
But for every tomorra!

'Tis glad I am
And glad I'll be
Knowin' you like
The likes o' me.

WHERE IS IRELAND?

No latitude or longitude
Can bound the Emerald Isle.
You'll find it off in Timbuktu
Or down along the Nile.

Wherever mothers stoop to smooth
A baby's touseled hair
And croon an Irish lullabye—
Ireland is there!

Wherever men are brave and true
And quick to take a stand
And proud to fight, if fight they must—
There is Ireland!

Wherever lad and lassie meet
A merry dance to share,
(Oh, echoes of the Blarney Stone!)
Ireland is there!

Wherever there's a song to sing,
A friend that needs a hand,
A cause to follow, come what may—
There is Ireland!

No latitude or longitude
Can bound the Emerald Isle.

You'll find it in a pair of eyes
You'll find it in a smile.

You'll know it by its laughter,
You'll know it by its tears,
You'll know it by the warmth of heart
That lasts through all the years.

THOMAS LANGAN

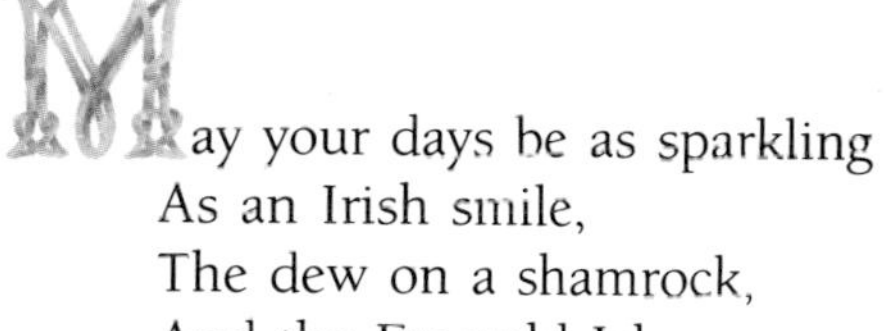

May your days be as sparkling
As an Irish smile,
The dew on a shamrock,
And the Emerald Isle.

Good times . . .
Good friends . . .
Good health to you . . .
And the luck of the Irish
In all that you do!

An Irish wish
From the heart of a friend—
"May good fortune be yours,
May your joys never end."

May your heart be light
Your cares be few
And may your wishes
All come true.

May the sound of happy music
And the lilt of Irish laughter
Fill your heart with gladness
That stays forever after.

Good cheer
Like a bit o' the morning sun
Good luck
To follow your days, each one
Good friends
To gladden your heart all through
Good health
And the finest of blessings for you.

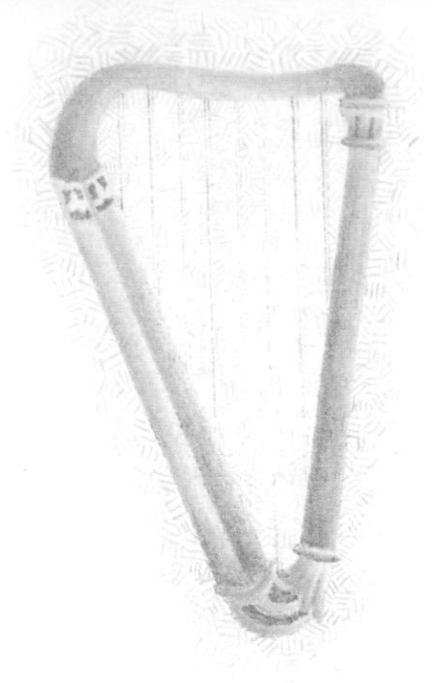

Sure as the shamrock's a beautiful
green
And Irish skies are blue—
Sure 'n the luck of the Irish is mine
Just knowin' the likes of you.

May your days be as bright
As the lakes of Killarney,
Your spirits be high
As the blue Irish sky,
May you walk in the path
Where the shamrocks are growin'
And blessings to you
For a wonderful day!

Leprechauns, castles
good luck and laughter
Lullabies, dreams
and love ever after.
Poems and songs
with pipes and drums
A thousand welcomes
when anyone comes . . .
That's the Irish for you!

In the name of dear Saint Patrick
This brings a loving prayer
May you forever be within
God's tender love and care—
May your heart be filled with happiness—
Your home be filled with laughter
And may the Holy Trinity
Bless your life forever after.

or each petal on the shamrock
This brings a wish your way—
Good health, good luck and happiness
For today and every day.

May the good Saint Patrick love you
And ask Our Lord to bless
You and all your dear ones
With health and happiness.

Here's to dear old Erin
That lovely Emerald Isle—
Here's to every colleen
And every colleen's smile—
Here's to Irish laughter—
And the Little People too—
Here's to dear old Erin
But most of all—here's to you!

May your days be very happy
May your life be free from cares
May Saint Patrick ask Our
  Blessed Lord
To answer all your prayers.

May our blessed good Saint Patrick
Whom we all so dearly love
Intercede and bring you
Many blessings from above.

May you have these . . .
the bright warm sun of happiness
the soft cool shade of joy
and many pleasures your whole life through.

ay you have only pleasant hours
To melt your cares away,
And the warmth of Irish laughter
To bring gladness to each day.

May your heart be light and happy
May your smile be big and wide
And may your pockets always have
A tinkle of gold inside.

Green are the hills of Ireland
And green they will always stay.
Warm are the blessings wished for you
And they'll always be that way.

What Is It to Be Irish?
How can you put the wonder of it into words? If a psychiatrist stretched himself out on his own warm couch after his last customer had gone home, and he dreamed of the man he himself would most like to be—well, he might be perfect, but he'd still only be half an Irishman on Saint Patrick's Day.

What Is It to Be Irish?
It is to have an angel in your mouth, turning your prose to poetry. It is to have the gift of tongues, to know the language of all living things. Does an Irishman pause and turn an ear to a tree? It is because on this day he wants to hear what one sleepy bud says to another as it opens its pale green hands to the warm sun of spring.

What Is It to Be Irish?
Oh, on this day it is music. Not just the cornet in the parading high school band, but the deep, deep music of living, the low, sad rhythms of eternity.

The Irishman hears the high song of the turning spheres, the dim lullaby of the worm in its cocoon. All the world is in tune, a tune that only he can hear.

What Is It to Be Irish?

It is to live the whole history of his race between a dawn and a dawn—the long wrongs, the bird swift joys, the endless hurt of his ancestors since the morning of time in a forgotten forest, the knock-at-his-heart that is part of his religion.

What Is It to Be Irish?

It's only the realization that he is descended from kings. It is the realization that he is a king himself, an empire on two feet striding in power, a strolling continent of awe.

What Is It to Be Irish?

Why on Saint Patrick's Day, to be Irish
is to know more glory, adventure,
magic, victory, exultation, gratitude and
gladness than any other man can
experience in a lifetime.

What Is It to Be Irish?

It is to walk in complete mystic
understanding with God for twenty-four
wonderful hours.

HAL BOYLE

ay Saint Patrick guard you wherever
you go and guide you in
whatever you do— and may his loving
protection be a blessing to you always.

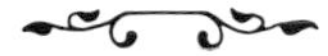

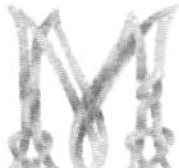ay you have many blessings
And wherever your path may wind
May every day that's coming
Be the bright and happy kind.

ay you have these blessings . . .
Good health to make life enjoyable
Good fortune to make it bright
And lots of happiness always
With everything going just right.

As lovely as Erin's rolling hills
Fair as its lakes and streams—
Joyful as its laughter—
Bright as all its dreams—
Lucky as its people
Happy as its leprechauns too—
May that be how each and every day
Will always be for you.

Have you ever been to Ireland
With its rolling hills so green?
Sure 'n it's the fairest land
That ever has been seen
And those green hills of Ireland
May be very far away
But they're close to every Irish heart
No matter what the day.